THIS IS A CARLTON BOOK

Text, illustrations and design copyright © 2008
Carlton Books Limited

This edition published by
Carlton Books Limited 2008
20 Mortimer Street
London W1T 3JW

A CIP catalogue record for this book is available from the British
Library.

ISBN 978-1-84732-070-4

Printed and bound in Singapore

Senior Executive Editor: Lisa Dyer
Senior Art Editor: Gulen Shevki-Taylor
Designer: Emma Wicks
Production: Kate Pimm

Your **Carbon Footprint** is the amount of carbon dioxide emitted
due to your daily activities – from washing a load of laundry to
driving to work. See www.carbonfootprint.com for ways to reduce
your impact on the environment.

the **little GREEN BOOK** of the

Home

SARAH CALLARD

250 TIPS FOR AN ECO LIFESTYLE

CARLTON BOOKS

Making changes to your home is one of the best ways to reduce your carbon footprint.
Whether it's a small step such as switching to energy-saving light bulbs, or a major commitment like converting to solar energy, you will be taking positive steps towards a greener future. This book looks at practical ways to help you 'green' your living space and is packed with useful information on how to incorporate green technology into your home.

1 CHANGE TO ENERGY-SAVING BULBS

This is one of the easiest ways to save energy immediately. Energy-saving bulbs, also known as compact fluorescent light bulbs (CFLs), use less than five times the energy of a standard incandescent bulb. They also last up to 12 times longer than incandescent bulbs, making them a cheaper option in the long run.

2 REMEMBER TO SWITCH OFF

Another very simple way to save energy at home is to always switch lights off when you leave a room. Incandescent bulbs are incredibly energy-inefficient and only convert around 5% of the energy they use into light, with the remainder being lost as heat.

3 USE TASK LIGHTING

Rather than using a single high-watt bulb to light a whole room, try using less-powerful, energy-efficient light bulbs to light specific areas for tasks such as reading or eating.

4 MAKE THE MOST OF NATURAL DAYLIGHT

Arrange your living space around the natural light that is available throughout the day. In the morning in the north-western countries, for example, use rooms that face south and east, and in the afternoon and evening use those facing west. Consider fitting a skylight in dark areas such as hallways and staircases.

5 NO NEED TO BE IN THE SPOTLIGHT

Avoid the temptation to introduce lots of spotlights in your home. These have become particularly popular in kitchens and bathrooms and although the halogen bulbs used in spots are more energy-efficient than incandescent bulbs, the sheer number makes them a less environmentally friendly option.

6 CHOOSE LED RATHER THAN HALOGEN SPOTLIGHTS

Light-emitting diodes (LEDs) are a fairly recent development in the energy-efficient lighting sector and they are the eco-alternative to halogen spotlighting. LEDs are now surpassing compact fluorescent light bulbs (CFLs) in efficiency. They are available in a wide range of colours and wattages so you won't have to compromise on ambience.

7

CHANGE YOUR MOST-USED BULBS

Start your move to low-energy lighting by switching the bulbs you use most to compact fluorescent light bulbs (CFLs). They can be applied anywhere that incandescent light bulbs are used and will generate the most savings in terms of energy and money. Any lighting left on for long periods will be much more cost-effective if the bulbs are energy-efficient.

8

HOW BRIGHT IS YOUR ENERGY-SAVING BULB?

Make sure you choose the right bulb for the right job: 7- to 9-watt energy-saving bulbs offer the same brightness as a 40-watt standard incandescent. The 11- to 15-watt bulbs are equivalent to 60-watt and 18- to 21-watt are the same as 100-watt bulbs.

9 RECYCLE YOUR LIGHT BULBS

Energy-saving bulbs contain around 5mg of mercury – a tiny amount but enough to ensure they are banned from landfill in the UK and in several US states. Make sure you take yours to a recycling centre or contact the manufacturer to find out the best way to recycle their light bulbs.

10 USE LESS LIGHT

Be aware of the number of lights you have on. If several light bulbs are controlled using one switch you could always take out some of the bulbs and replace when necessary. Use individual spotlights and sidelights instead of switching all the lights on at once.

11 TURN DOWN THE THERMOSTAT

This is one of the best ways to save energy at home. The thermostat should be set at around 19°C (66°F) for a comfortable temperature. You will also save up to 10% of your heating bills simply by turning the thermostat down by 1°C (34°F).

12 FIT RADIATOR VALVES

Fitting radiator valves is an excellent way to control the temperature throughout the house rather than wasting energy heating rooms that don't necessarily need it all the time. Cheap to buy and easy to install, adding radiator valves could cut your energy use by around 5%.

ADD A ROOM THERMOSTAT

A room thermostat will increase the efficiency of your central heating system. If used in conjunction with other controls such as radiator valves this could reduce your energy use by as much as 15%. Just make sure you don't install a room thermostat in the same room as a radiator with valves because they will counteract each other.

KEEP BEDROOMS COOLER

Make proper use of your radiator valves and save energy. Although a temperature of 19°C (66°F) is recommended for living spaces, bedrooms can be cooler at around 15°C (59°F). Remember to set different temperatures for rooms depending on how much they are used.

15 INSULATE BEHIND RADIATORS

Fit a sheet of aluminium foil or insulation on the wall behind the radiator and this will help to reduce energy waste, particularly if the radiator is on an outside wall. It is also possible to buy rigid reflective radiator panels that can be used without having to take the radiator off the wall – they simply slip into the gap between the wall and the radiator.

16 DON'T PUT CURTAINS IN FRONT OF RADIATORS

Doing this simply funnels the heat away from the room and out of the window. Crop the curtains so they fit snugly onto the windowsill above the radiators and make sure they are lined for extra insulation.

17 FIT WOODEN SHELVES OVER RADIATORS

Putting a shelf above your radiators will force the warm air to circulate around the room instead of going straight up to the ceiling. If the radiator is under a window, the shelf will also stop the heat travelling behind the curtains.

18 CHOOSE A WOOD BURNER, NOT AN OPEN FIRE

If you really want a solid-fuel fire in your home, make sure it's a wood-burning stove rather than an open fire, which is very energy inefficient, losing around 85% of the heat up the chimney. Make sure you use locally sourced, sustainably managed wood that is carbon neutral.

19

MAKE YOUR OWN LOGS

If you have a wood burner, invest in a log maker. These practical devices turn old newspapers into 'logs' that burn for around an hour. Cheap and easy to use, they provide roughly one log per newspaper. Use extra newspaper and kindling to get the fire started.

20

USE A CHIMNEY BALLOON

To stop draughts coming in from the chimney, invest in a chimney balloon (www.chimneyballoon.com). They sit about a foot up above the fireplace opening and you can easily fit one yourself. Chimney balloons stop draughts, heat loss, soot and debris, and have just enough ventilation to keep the chimney dry.

21 PUT ON AN EXTRA LAYER

Before turning up, or even turning on, your heating, wear an extra sweater and socks and save energy and money. Keep a cosy throw on the sofa, too, and cuddle up in it on really cold nights.

22 GET RID OF THE ELECTRIC BLANKET

As well as the health and safety concerns associated with electric blankets, they also use unnecessary energy. Instead of switching one on, fill a hot-water bottle, use thick organic cotton sheets and woollen blankets to make the bed feel warmer, and wrap up in organic cotton thermals.

WARM UP NATURALLY

Instead of turning up the heating, invest in (or make your own) wheat or rice packs. These are a great way to warm up without using very much energy – just place the bags in a microwave for a couple of minutes and enjoy. They have the added benefit of easing pain, and are much more energy-friendly than heating pads.

INCREASE YOUR LOFT INSULATION

Heating is responsible for more than 75% of the energy consumption of the average household and around half of heat loss in a typical home is through the loft (attic) and walls. The recommended depth for loft insulation is a depth of 270 mm (10 in), which could save about a third of your heating costs.

25 USE NATURAL MATERIALS FOR INSULATION

Natural insulation materials (such as the kind made from fire-retarded recycled newspaper or sheep's wool) have added benefits as well as a lower environmental impact. Being natural, they are biodegradable and safe to handle. They also help to keep humidity stable because they absorb moisture when it's humid and release it when the air is drier.

26 ADD CAVITY WALL INSULATION

Cavity wall insulation is one of the most cost-effective energy-efficiency measures you can carry out in your home. It reduces heat loss through the external walls by around 60% and is relatively cheap to install. However, it must be carried out by an expert.

27

DOUBLE-GLAZE YOUR WINDOWS

Around 20% of the heat lost from an average family home occurs through single-glazed windows and badly insulated window frames. By fitting double-glazing this loss can be reduced by more than half. If you can't afford to replace all your windows, double glaze the ones in the rooms you heat the most.

28

DRAUGHT-PROOF DOORS AND WINDOWS

Around 20% of the heat in the average home is lost through ventilation and draughts. Keep the warmth in by adding draught excluders to doors and windows. Fittings are available from most DIY stores, making this an inexpensive and easy way to save energy.

29 USE HEAVY-LINED CURTAINS

Keep the heat in by drawing your curtains at dusk. Close them when it gets dark and consider adding a lining to further reduce heat loss through windows. If they are unlined, another option is to get an inexpensive second pair of curtains to act as lining material.

30 SHUTTER UP

Wooden shutters on windows are excellent insulators, along with the added advantage that they look elegant. Shutters could be a good option if you don't have double-glazing. If you live in an old house, check that you don't already have shutters – they may have been boarded into the wall.

31

PUT A JACKET ON YOUR HOT-WATER CYLINDER

Save energy by insulating your hot-water cylinder by fitting a 'jacket' around it, which could cut heat loss by over 75%. If you already have a jacket on your cylinder make sure it's at least 75 mm (3 in) thick for optimum energy saving.

32

LAG YOUR PIPES

Insulating the pipes in your central heating system when they pass through parts of the house that you don't need to heat such as the loft is a good way to save energy. Insulation material for a standard 15-mm (½-in) pipe is cheap and effective.

33 COVER YOUR LETTERBOX

Valuable heat and energy are lost through draughts around the home. One of the main areas where heat escapes from your home is through the letterbox (mail slot). Save valuable energy, especially if you don't have a porch area, by fitting a cover with flexible bristles or a magnetic seal that create a constant seal.

34 CHOOSE WOOD, NOT PVC FOR DOUBLE-GLAZING

If you decide to fit double-glazing, make sure you use wood for the frames rather than PVC or even aluminium. The energy and toxins created during the manufacture of PVC make it an environmental no-no and it's also extremely difficult to recycle.

35 BLOCK UP DRAUGHTY FLOORBOARDS

Draughts caused by gaps in wooden floorboards waste energy and can make your home feel cold and uncomfortable. There are various ways to block up these draughts, including non-toxic sealants, underlays or hardboard, which will save you money as well as reducing energy.

36 CHOOSE WIND-OPERATED TO REDUCE CONDENSATION

A wind-operated extractor (exhaust) fan is the best way to resolve any condensation problems in rooms such as bathrooms and kitchens. They reduce the need to open windows and are powered simply by the difference in pressure so no energy is required at all, unlike an electric extractor.

37 GREEN YOUR ROOF

This may sound a little extreme but turf-covered roofs are becoming more popular and are now easier to put together. Planting turf on your roof creates natural insulation, thereby saving energy, improves air quality and has the added bonus of encouraging biodiversity. You will, however, need to ensure that your roof is strong enough to support the weight of the turf or plants when saturated with rainwater or snowfall.

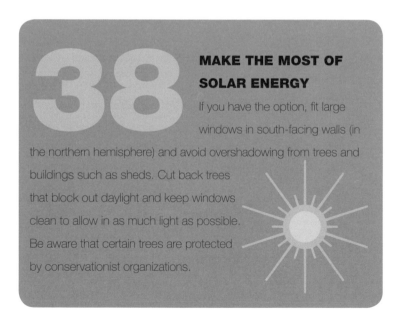

38 MAKE THE MOST OF SOLAR ENERGY

If you have the option, fit large windows in south-facing walls (in the northern hemisphere) and avoid overshadowing from trees and buildings such as sheds. Cut back trees that block out daylight and keep windows clean to allow in as much light as possible. Be aware that certain trees are protected by conservationist organizations.

39

HEAT YOUR HOT WATER WITH SOLAR ENERGY

Solar hot-water heating is now quite a practical way to create your own hot water from the sun's energy. Today's solar water heating panels may be integrated into most types of hot water systems, including combination boilers, and can provide you with around of third of your hot-water needs.

40 BUILD A CONSERVATORY

Building a conservatory or sunroom is a fantastic way to make the most of solar energy. It's also a cheaper option for insulating your house because it acts as a protective zone between the house and the outside, trapping the sun's heat and cutting heat loss.

41

FIT A DOMESTIC WIND TURBINE

This may seem an elaborate idea but if you live in an exposed, windy area, it could be a good way to create at least some of the energy you need for heating and lighting your home. Small domestic wind turbines are available now from many DIY outlets, and can be mounted on your roof.

42

WARM UP WITH A GEOTHERMAL HEAT PUMP

Geothermal heating is one way of using a renewable energy source to provide much of your heating needs and it is becoming a more realistic option. Similar to ordinary heat pumps, they use the earth's heat from the ground instead of outside air to provide heating, air conditioning and, in most cases, hot water. It's estimated you can save 2 to 8 tonnes of carbon dioxide emissions each year via a geothermal heat pump.

43

OPEN YOUR CURTAINS DURING DAYLIGHT HOURS

Make the most of natural daylight by opening the curtains wide in the day and getting rid of light-diffusing nets or sheers. This saves the energy that you may have used in lighting the space unnecessarily and makes the most of natural solar energy.

44

UNBLOCK DRAINS NATURALLY

Instead of using chemical products to clear blocked drains, try pouring down a solution of 4 tablespoons bicarbonate of soda (baking soda) and 50 ml (2 fl oz) vinegar in boiling water. If you do this regularly, it should help to prevent your drains from getting blocked again.

45 OPT OUT OF THE WASHING UP WITH A DISHWASHER

Instead of washing all your dishes by hand, you should use a dishwasher if you have space. Research comparing handwashing to dishwashers found that dishwashers use just half the energy and one-sixth of the water of than is used when washing dishes by hand.

46 USE ECO-FRIENDLY CLEANING PRODUCTS

Conventional cleaning products such as laundry detergents and household cleaners can leak chemical solvents and toxins into the environment. Common ingredients include petroleum-based surfactants derived from non-renewable sources, which have also been linked to health problems including cancer and hormone-disruption. A recent study also found a strong link between asthma and cleaning products.

47 WASH WITH SOAP NUTS

Soap nuts grow on trees in India and Nepal and their shells contain saponin, a natural soap. Instead of using detergent put 6–8 soap-nut shells in a cotton bag or knotted sock and place them in the drum of your washing machine on a 40°C (120°F) cycle.

48 CLEAN UP WITH BICARBONATE OF SODA

Bicarbonate of soda, also known as baking soda, makes a versatile household cleaner. Use it to get rid of smells by placing a small bowl in the kitchen or refrigerator. Shake it onto carpets before vacuuming to freshen them up and sprinkle on dishes or in the bottom of the dishwasher to absorb food odours and give crockery cleaning an extra boost.

SWITCH TO E-CLOTHS

Avoid using plastic scourers and sponges to clean your dishes and invest in a set of e-cloths. These are microfibre cleaning cloths that neither contain nor require chemicals. They are designed to remove the surface layer of dirt, leaving bacteria without anywhere to grow, and you only need to use water with them.

CLEANING GOES FAIRTRADE

Certified fairtrade cleaning cloths made from a circular-knitted natural cotton yarn are now available. They are unbleached and can be used for cleaning, doing dishes or dry dusting. One variety, made by Minky in the UK, uses cotton grown by a cooperative of small-scale farmers in Mali before being spun by accredited suppliers in Europe.

51

GREEN YOUR WASHING MACHINE NATURALLY

To give your washing machine a good clean, add a generous handful of bicarbonate of soda (baking soda) to the drum of the machine and put it on a hot wash cycle. This should get rid of any nasty smells caused by detergent build-up; done regularly it will also help to keep your machine in good condition.

52

USE ECO-FRIENDLY CLOTHES DETERGENT

One of the most un-environmentally friendly aspects of washing our clothes is the type of detergent we use. Conventional washing powders contain chemicals such as whitening agents and surfactants that have a detrimental impact on the environment. Choose eco products such as Ecover, Bio-D or Sonett.

53 AVOID AIR FRESHENERS

A recent study found that many air fresheners contain phthalates, which have been linked with health scares such as cancer. Additionally, many air fresheners are 'plug-ins', which use energy on a constant basis. Research indicates that a single plug-in is responsible for generating 13.5 kg (29 lb) of CO_2 a year.

54 MAKE YOUR OWN HOME SCENTS

Instead of relying on synthetic air fresheners, make your own. Try adding a few drops of your favourite essential oil to filtered water in a spray container and use it to spritz areas that often need freshening up, such as the kitchen and cloakroom.

55 GIVE A VINEGAR SPARKLE

Avoid harsh chemicals and use vinegar to clean your home instead. It can be added to water and used to clean floors and surfaces in place of disinfectants, removing a dull, greasy films. Add half a cup of vinegar to 2 litres (½ gallon) of water. It also gets rid of hard water stains on glasses and gives them a real shine.

56 BE LEMON FRESH

Get rid of strong smells in the refrigerator by placing half a lemon inside to absorb the odours. Lemon also works in the microwave – just put a couple of slices in a microwave-proof bowl of cold water and switch the power on for a few minutes.

57 CLEAN UP WITH LEMON

Fresh or bottled, lemon juice makes a fantastic natural cleaner. Bleach wooden chopping boards by rubbing them with lemon juice and leave overnight before rinsing. Lemon juice also removes lime scale (mineral deposits) from taps (faucets) and can be used to clean worktops and surfaces.

58 AVOID DRYING CLOTHES ON RADIATORS

Clothes drying on radiators prevents the heat reaching the rest of the room, creates damp and provides good growing conditions for mould. Instead, try to dry clothes outside whenever possible, or alternatively use a clothes airer in a room that can be well ventilated.

59 BRING A SPARKLE TO GLASS WITH VINEGAR

Mix up equal parts of vinegar and warm water to create an ideal window-cleaning solution. Apply the mixture to the window with a piece of scrunched-up newspaper and rub. There's no need to worry – any vinegary smells will disappear once the window is dry!

60 PURIFY WITH HOUSEPLANTS

Many indoor plants not only look nice but they also act as natural air conditioners. Research has shown that they can remove up to 87% of indoor pollution in 24 hours. Draecana, spider plants, peace lilies and Areca palms all act as air purifiers. Placing a yucca in the bathroom has also been found to be a good way to neutralize any bad smells from the toilet.

61 MAKE YOUR BATHROOM SHINE

To give your toilet a really good clean, drop a couple of denture-cleaning tablets into the bowl and leave overnight. Another cleaning tip is to add a can of cola to the bowl and leave overnight before scrubbing and flushing away.

62 NATURAL MOTH REPELLENTS

Conventional mothballs often contain chemicals that have been found to be toxic and even carcinogenic. Buy or, better still, make your own natural mothballs. Make sachets of fabric and fill with dried lavender or herbs scented with essential oils. Moths don't like lavender or cedarwood.

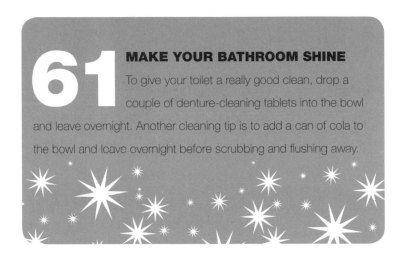

63

CHOOSE POWDERED DETERGENT

Liquid detergents generally contain a great deal more surfactant than powders and usually they also come packaged in plastic. Surfactants, (commonly used in household and bodycare products), have been found to be slow to biodegrade as well as damaging to plants and animals. Both powder and liquid compacts use less detergent per wash than the other forms.

64

GIVE YOUR UNDIES A NATURAL FRAGRANCE

Add small packages or envelopes of homemade herb and essential oil mixtures to your underwear drawer to give a pleasant fragrance. These sachets can also be placed in shoes and trainers to ward off bad odours. Try geranium and lavender. You can also sprinkle on cotton wool balls.

65 DON'T BUY ANTIBACTERIAL CLEANING PRODUCTS

Some studies have found that antibacterial products actually contribute to the increase in 'superbugs' and can cause dry skin and hand eczema. Don't believe the hype: avoid products containing the antibacterial ingredient triclosan. Soap and hot water will kill germs just as effectively.

66 SWITCH TO ECOBALLS

Stop using detergent in your washing machine by switching to reusable laundry balls such as Eco-balls. They last for up to 1,000 washes and work by ionizing the water via the agitation of ceramic granules within the perforated balls. And you don't need to add fabric softener because they also help to soften clothes washed in hard water.

AVOID FABRIC CONDITIONERS

Some liquid fabric softeners have been found to contain formaldehyde, which is a known carcinogen. Other chemicals found in conventional fabric conditioners have been linked to skin irritation and even cancer. Instead, add 125 ml (4 fl oz) white distilled vinegar or bicarbonate of soda (baking soda) to the rinse.

CLEAN UP WITH SALT

Salt can be used for a number of cleaning tasks around the home, reducing the need for chemical products. Use it to reduce smells by sprinkling around the inside of the garbage bin. It will also remove stains from china and whitens discoloured wooden draining or bread boards.

69

MAKE YOUR OWN FURNITURE POLISH

For a green alternative to conventional furniture polish sprays, mix grated beeswax and turpentine. Heat in a bowl over hot water until the beeswax dissolves. Add a few drops of essential oil such as lavender or pine and use a soft cloth to rub it into furniture.

70

FIGHT MOULD WITH BORAX

Borax is a naturally occurring mineral that is kind to the environment. It can irritate skin and eyes, however, so take care when using it. Sprinkle it onto a damp cloth and wipe down bathtubs and showers. It also inhibits mould growth, so use it to wash down walls, or alternatively leave a thick paste of water and Borax on the affected area overnight before brushing off and rinsing.

71 SODA WATER FOR STAINS

Instead of reaching for a chemical cocktail when spills and stains occur on carpets, try soda water or carbonated water. They will do the job just as well without emitting the chemicals caused by lots of conventional products.

72 DON'T BUY INTO DRY-CLEANING

Try to avoid purchasing clothes that have to be dry-cleaned or hand-wasn instead. The chemicals used in dry-cleaning carry traces of tetrachlorethylene, which has been linked to dizziness, headaches and fatigue, as well as being a potential carcinogen.

73

NATURAL HOME FRAGRANCE

Use bunches of herbs or flowers, ideally cut from your own garden, and essential oils to fragrance your home rather than synthetic air fresheners. Light soy candles and try making your own potpourri using dried herbs such as lavender, along with dried rose petals and camomile flowers.

74

LEAVE YOUR SHOES AT THE DOOR

Cut back on the use of household cleaners by leaving your shoes at the door. This reduces dust by an estimated 60%, making your home a cleaner and healthier environment. Open windows regularly to let in fresh air and to get rid of nasty smells.

75

GET YOURSELF A MOP

A traditional string mop lasts longer than cheaper foam versions. You can buy replacement heads for some mops but most may be washed in the washing machine – put the mop in a pillowcase first to protect your machine. Another green way to wash floors is to tie a floor-cloth to a brush. Wash the cloth afterwards and reuse.

76

REDUCE THE NUMBER OF CLEANING PRODUCTS

Do you really need a separate product for each job? Streamline your cleaning cupboard to just a few items and use natural alternatives such as vinegar and lemon for household cleaning jobs rather than relying on chemical products.

41

77

USE SODA CRYSTALS FOR HOUSEHOLD CLEANING

For many years soda crystals, also known as washing soda, has been used for cleaning. It is biodegradable and doesn't contain phosphates, enzymes or bleach. Soda crystals are suitable for cleaning work tops, lavatories and mirrors as well as unblocking drains and pipes.

78

TRY BRUSHES FOR DISHES

Rather than buying scourers with plastic handles, buy longer-lasting wooden varieties with natural fibre bristles. Look out for brushes with replaceable heads. They will no doubt cost more but they will last longer and have far less impact on the environment.

79

CUT BACK ON DISPOSAL CLOTHS

Avoid wastage from disposable scourers and kitchen cloths by buying cotton cloths that can be washed and reused. Make your own scourers from the nylon mesh bags that fruit comes in. These can be stuffed inside each other and tied up to form a ball.

80

MAKE A LIST BEFORE YOU GO SHOPPING

Get into the habit of planning the week's meals and writing a shopping list before you go out. This helps to reduce the amount of waste food you have and also saves you money, as long as you stick to it and don't get lured into impulse purchases. It's best not to shop when you're feeling hungry!

81 HAVE A FLASK ON HAND

Make sure your home has at least one thermos flask that can be used to hold hot drinks and soups. This will help reduce waste from plastic cups and takeout food containers. A flask can also be a good idea if you work from home because it saves having to brew up fresh cups.

82 TEACH YOUR FAMILY TO COOK

If you are the main cook, encourage the other members of your family to learn how to put together a few basic meals. Cooking from fresh ingredients saves money and resources, particularly packaging. It may also mean that you get to have a night or two away from the kitchen.

83 ~~BUY ORGANIC MILK~~
BUY DAIRY FREE MILK

Organic milk takes three times less energy to produce than the non-organic version. This is mainly due to the energy used in the production of the fertilizers employed in non-organic milk production. Various studies have also found that organic milk has more health benefits with higher levels of antioxidants.

84 GROUP SHOPPING

Join forces with friends and buy in bulk to cut down on packaging. Certain groceries, such as cereals, rice and pasta, can be bought in bulk from wholesalers, as long as you meet their minimum order – then it's just up to you to divide it up. This is a great way to reduce packaging and save money.

85

HOW FAR DOES YOUR FOOD TRAVEL?

When you are shopping for groceries, keep an eye out for food miles and reduce yours whenever possible. You might be surprised to discover that the apples you regularly buy are flown all the way from New Zealand. Try to buy local food whenever possible.

86

SHOP FROM HOME

Do your food shopping online to cut down on carbon emissions caused by driving to the supermarket. Recent research has revealed that getting your groceries delivered by an online delivery service is around 30% more energy efficient than travelling to the store itself to shop.

87 ORDER A VEGETABLE BOX

Instead of driving to the supermarket for your weekly groceries, arrange for an organic vegetable box to be delivered to your door. This has the combined benefits of supporting a local producer (check that's where the food comes from), helping to reduce chemicals used in conventional farming and reducing emissions caused by trips to the shops.

88 SIZE MATTERS

When buying new gadgets for the home such as can openers, only purchase one big enough for the job in question. Larger items use more resources during their manufacture. The only time a larger gadget is preferable is when it lasts twice as long as this saves resources in the long run.

89 DRINK TAP WATER

Tap water costs a fraction of the price of bottled water and creates no waste. If you are concerned about the chlorine used to disinfect tap water, simply fill a jug and place it in the refrigerator to allow the chlorine to evaporate. Remember to keep the water covered and replace it every 24 hours.

90 GROW YOUR OWN VEG

Eliminate food miles and get back to nature by growing your own vegetables. Even if you don't have a garden you can still grow tomatoes and herbs inside in pots or in growbags. Homegrown also means you can avoid the packaging that often comes with bought groceries.

91

AVOID HIGH-TECH CARTONS WHENEVER POSSIBLE

Try not to buy juice, milk and soup in cartons because they are extremely difficult to recycle, being made from a mixture of different materials. They do, however, take less energy to produce and transport than tin cans, and any you do buy can be reused in the garden as plant pots for seedlings.

92

MILK TO YOUR DOOR

Getting fresh milk delivered in reusable then recyclable glass bottles is the best way to buy milk. It cuts down on plastic packaging and saves you the hassle of lugging pints of milk home from the shops. Glass milk bottles are generally used around 40 times and before being recycled.

93 COTTON ALTERNATIVES

Regular cotton farming can be hard on the environment – cotton being the most chemical dependent crop in the world. However, organic cotton is grown without chemicals, using materials and methods that have a low impact on our environment. Bamboo is another good choice for towels as it is very absorbent and the organic process requires no chemicals and less water than even organic cotton growth.

94 COMPOST YOUR KITCHEN WASTE

Reduce waste by composting kitchen scraps and other waste. Put leftover food and other waste such as used tea bags, peelings and coffee grounds to good use with a composter. Even if you don't have a garden, you can compost kitchen waste in a small wormery.

95 USE YOUR LEFTOVERS

One-third of food ends up getting thrown away without being composted, so don't over-buy in the first place and use up leftovers by incorporating them into new dishes. When mixed with other materials in landfill sites, food waste can produce polluting liquids along with methane gases which contribute to the greenhouse effect.

96 EAT SEASONALLY

The choice of fruit and vegetables at most supermarkets is staggering. Whatever the time of year, you can pretty much eat what you want. This exotice choice is the result of miles of airfreighting and tonnes of CO_2 emissions. Instead buy local produce from farm shops and markets, which cuts emissions and supports local producers.

97 CONSUME LESS MEAT

Encourage your household to eat less meat. A report by the United Nations Food and Agriculture Organisation revealed that the livestock sector generates more greenhouse gas emissions than transport. Almost a fifth of climate-changing greenhouse gases come from livestock production and the growing of their feed crops.

98 BUY FAIRTRADE

Whoever does the household shopping should get into the habit of buying products that carry the FLO's International Fairtrade mark. This logo certifies that the producers are getting a fair price for the goods including sustainable production and a premium to be invested in social or economic development projects.

99 AVOID PLASTIC ALTOGETHER

Don't fill your cupboards with unwanted plastic shopping bags that you feel too guilty to dispose of. Invest in a couple of reusable bags, preferably made from a biodegradable material such as hessian, that can be used over and over again. If you must use plastic food storage bags, wash and reuse them as many times as you can.

100 GET ONYA BAG

One of the main problems with reusable shopping bags is we forget to take them shopping! The Onya Bag is an ideal choice because it is superstrong, folds down to a tiny pouch and can be clipped onto your bag or purse (see www.onyabags.com.au).

101

AVOID TEFLON PANS

There is growing concern that over-heated Teflon and other non-stick pans release toxic fumes; also concern about the pollution caused during the manufacturing process of Teflon. Use stainless steel saucepans or iron-bottomed pots instead.

102

SWITCH OFF THE POWER

Kitchen appliances are some of the biggest energy consumers while on standby. Microwaves in particular often have features such as clocks that end up using more energy than the actual cooking process so switch off at the main outlet when they are not in use.

103 FEEL THE PRESSURE

Save energy while you are cooking by using a pressure cooker. They work by cooking food under high pressure in a short period of time, thereby speeding up the cooking process and saving energy. Also, try to cook bigger batches of dishes like soups and stews and freeze extra portions for future meals.

104 KEEP YOUR REFRIGERATOR ON TOP FORM

Encourage your refrigerator to be as energy-efficient as possible by keeping it clean and well positioned. Make sure you regularly dust down the coils at the back – dusty coils can waste up to 30% extra electricity.

105

STEER CLEAR OF SIX-PACKS

Try to avoid buying cans of drinks held together by plastic yokes. Many of these end up in our oceans, where they can get trapped around the beaks and necks of birds and mammals. If you do find yourself with a plastic yoke to dispose of, make sure you cut the yokes first.

106

REUSE OLD FOOD CONTAINERS

Rather than throwing them out, recycle old food containers such as ice-cream tubs and jam jars to store food leftover foods and small household items. Jars with screw-top lids are a great way to store dried goods such as lentils, as well as old screws and nails.

107 REACH FOR THE MICROWAVE

If you are simply reheating food rather than cooking a meal it is more energy-efficient to use the microwave rather than the oven. However, don't use the microwave to defrost food: think ahead and put it in the refrigerator to defrost overnight before you need it.

108 CHOOSE WOOD IN THE KITCHEN

When buying utensils for your kitchen try to avoid plastic wherever possible. Wooden washing-up brushes and stainless steel utensils are widely available and a greener alternative to plastic, which has a big environmental impact during its production and disposal.

109

DON'T BUY PLASTIC FOR PICNICS

It may be tempting to invest in a brightly coloured picnic set for days out or simply for use in the garden, but from an environmental perspective you should avoid buying plastic if at all possible. A picnic is a good reason to bring out old crockery and cups that you might otherwise throw away.

110

NO NEED FOR PLASTIC WRAP TO STORE FOOD

The production of the polyethylene used to produce plastic wrap is wasteful in terms of energy, raw materials and pollution. There is also research to prove that some of the chemicals found in plastic wrap may actually leach into foods causing health problems, so try to avoid it.

111 USE RECYCLED KITCHEN PAPER TOWELS

When buying kitchen roll make sure that you look for products with a high-recycled content, preferably 100%. This will help to reduce the energy used to produce kitchen roll or towels as far less is required for recycled paper. Also, look out for unbleached varieties to reduce the use of chlorine bleach, a pollutant.

112 GROW YOUR OWN FLAVOURFUL HERBS

Even if you're not at all green-fingered or don't have a garden you can still grow a few herbs in small containers to help to liven up your diet. Indoor pots (try recycling cans and yogurt pots) may be used to grow herbs such as basil, thyme and parsley – you'll be saving energy and reducing emissions, too.

113 REDUCE FOOD WASTE AT HOME

Make sure you are not throwing away lots of leftover food by following a few simple rules. Always try to incorporate leftovers into other meals, and freeze or bottle surplus fruit and vegetables. Grind leftover bread into breadcrumbs to make fat balls for birds.

114 DON'T USE PLASTIC CUPS FOR SPECIAL EVENTS

If you're having a party or a special event and need extra cups, don't be tempted into buying 'disposable' plastic ones that are simply destined for landfill. Many off licences (liquor stores) and supermarkets offer a glass hire service, which is a far greener option.

115

BUY YOUR FRUIT AND VEG LOOSE

Avoid purchasing fruit and vegetables that come pre-packaged in lots of plastic. Mcuh of it is totally unnecessary and simply adds to household waste. Visit shops and food markets where you can buy produce loose and avoid all packaging by taking along your own reusable shopping bags.

116

CUTLERY OF STEEL

Stainless steel has a high proportion of recycled content – on average around 80%. Items made from stainless steel can be melted down and reformed into a new product, which makes it a good green choice for kitchen equipment such as cutlery; it is also hardwearing.

117

USE RECYCLED FOIL

If you can't do without aluminium foil (which has a major environmental impact during its production), make sure you use 100% recycled aluminium foil. This product can be recycled over and over again. Producing recycled foil uses 95% less energy than is used when making primary aluminium.

118

DECORATE WITH ECO PAINTS

Reduce your carbon footprint by up to 30 kg (66 lb) by decorating with eco-paint. Paint production is known to be extremely inefficient in terms of energy use, with the manufacture of 1 tonne of paint producing up to 10 tonnes of waste, much of it toxic.

119 PAINT A BETTER PICTURE

Traditional household paints aren't good for your health. In general, they are made using petrochemical-derived ingredients. These solvents contain volatile organic compounds (VOCs) that have been linked with health scares such as cancer as well as respiratory problems, headaches and eye, nose and throat irritation. Water-based paints contain less of these than oil-based.

120 SAND, DON'T STRIP!

The least environmentally harmful way to remove old paint is to sand it down. Paint-stripping chemicals are damaging to the environment and have been linked with health concerns. Keep the room well ventilated and throw paint shavings away in a sealed container.

121   ALWAYS RECYCLE UNWANTED PAINT

Never throw unwanted paint away down a drain. See if you can pass it on to any community groups or schools who may be able to use it. Otherwise it should be taken to a recycling centre, where it will almost certainly end up on landfill.

122   COMPOST LEFTOVER NATURAL PAINTS

Natural paints are a more environmentally friendly option for a number of reasons. They have a lower environmental impact during their manufacture, they are made from plant-based ingredients rather than petrochemicals and they are mostly biodegradable, some being suitable for composting once they have dried out.

123 FURNISH WITH FSC CERTIFIED WOOD

When buying any wooden furniture or flooring for your home ensure that it carries the Forest Stewardship Council (FSC) stamp. This means that the wood meets the criteria for environmental, social and economic sustainability and that it is not a product of illegal logging.

124 USE NATURAL FLOORING

To avoid emissions given off by synthetic materials in conventional flooring, choose a natural option such as wood or bamboo. Wood flooring should be certified by the Forest Stewardship Council (FSC) to ensure it comes from a sustainable source. Natural fibres such as sisal, hemp and coir also make good natural floor materials.

125 GIVE YOUR HOME SOME ECO CHIC

Add colour and texture to your home with the addition of eco-friendly upholstery. Cushions made from recycled vintage shirts and ties and throws of 100% recycled wool will give your home a new look without harming the environment. For ideas visit www.ecocentric.co.uk.

126 RECLAIMED WOODEN FLOORS

If you decide to lay a wooden floor or you need to replace some of your existing floorboards, look out for wooden boards in reclamation yards and salvage stores. This is a great way to give wood a new lease of life and ensures your floor has lots of character.

127

LIVING WITHOUT SYNTHETICS

Carpets, paint and vinyl wallpaper can all emit volatile organic compounds (VOCs) and other pollutants that have been linked with asthma and other health concerns. Natural materials are a greener and healthier choice for decorating your home.

128

MAKE SURE YOUR WORKTOPS ARE RECYCLED

If you are fitting a new kitchen, look out for recycled units and fittings. Worktops made from 100% post-consumer coffee cups or recycled mobile (cell) phones are now available, as are cupboard doors created from recycled yogurt pots. Sinks made from 80% recycled steel, which is endlessly recyclable, are also available.

129 BOOST YOUR INSULATION WITH NATURAL PAINT

Natural paint manufacturers have now developed wall-insulating paint, designed to help regulate the temperature inside the house throughout the year. Ecos Organic Paints (www.ecosorganicpaints. com) claim their version will save between 10–30% of energy lost through walls.

130 SWITCH TO A NATURAL FIBRE MATTRESS

We spend about a third of our lives sleeping so investing in a good-quality mattress makes sense. Cheaper mattresses are often produced from synthetic foam, and can contain formaldehyde, pesticides and other chemicals. Mattresses made from natural materials are less likely to cause allergic reactions. If a new mattress has a strange smell that lasts for weeks, call the manufacturer and request an exchange.

131

CHOOSE A WOODEN SLATTED BASE FOR YOUR BED

A wooden bed base not only enables air to circulate around your mattress, it is, of course, made from a sustainable material. Look out for products that carry the Forest Stewardship Council (FSC) mark certifying that the wood is from a sustainable managed source or wood that has been reclaimed.

132

ANIMAL DUVETS ARE GREENER

The most eco-friendly duvet fillings are made from goose feathers or down. From an ethical point of view check that the feathers have been gathered from the ground rather than plucked from a live bird. An even more animal-friendly option is to use woollen blankets and organic cotton sheets.

133 CHOOSE ORGANIC COTTON BEDDING

Pesticides are banned in organic cotton production so make sure you choose organic sheets and towels. The number of cotton farmers suffering acute pesticide poisoning each year is between 25 and 77 million worldwide according to a report published earlier in 2007 by the Environmental Justice Foundation (EJF) and the Pesticide Action Network (PAN).

134 REDISCOVER CORK TILES

Cork is a sustainable, natural material that comes from the base of the cork tree. Biodegradable and non-polluting, it is an ideal material for use on floors and walls. Cork is made up of millions of air pockets so it also makes a good insulation material, keeping warmth in and noise out.

135 PICK A NATURAL VARNISH FOR FLOORS

If you have a wooden floor make sure you use a natural varnish to seal it rather than a solvent-based product that may emit pollutants. Natural varnishes contain plant-derived resins and oils and allow the wood to breathe. Wooden furniture and fittings can be finished with beeswax or linseed oil.

136 NOT SO FANTASTIC HOME PLASTICS

Whether it's food containers in the kitchen or toothbrush holders in the bathroom, plastic should be avoided whenever possible. It is a by-product of the energy-intensive, high-polluting petroleum industry. Plastics can also emit harmful vapours known as VOCs and some types are extremely difficult if not impossible to recycle. AFM SafeCoat in the US and Ecos Organic in the UK are both good zero-VOC paint brands.

137 CUT OUT CUT FLOWERS

Many cut flowers are flown thousands of miles from large-scale producers in Kenya to Europe, or in South America to North America. This creates emissions caused by 'flower miles' made worse by the fact that the flowers have to be refrigerated during transit. Flower producers have also been criticised for their high use of agrochemicals.

138 USE WOOD IN THE BATHROOM

Avoid having lots of unnecessary plastic accessories in your bathroom. Choose wooden soap dishes and toothpaste holders and look for wooden body brushes and natural loofahs rather than plastic varieties. These have the advantage of being sustainable and biodegradable.

139

WRAP UP IN ORGANIC TOWELS

Unbleached organic cotton towels are the most eco-friendly way to dry off in the bathroom. Cotton production uses vast amounts of pesticides and is a major global pollutant. Buying organic benefits the environment and reduces your exposure to potential pesticide residues.

140

GO GREEN FOR FURNITURE

When you are looking for new furniture make sure you pick pieces made from natural, sustainable materials such as untreated wood certified by the Forest Stewardship Council (FSC). If you are renovating furniture, ensure that you use plant-based paints and finishes.

141 RECYCLE AT HOME

Where possible, recycle your waste. Paper, plastic, glass and metal can all be recycled and most are collected by doorstep recycling schemes. Remember also to buy products with some recycled content, such as toilet paper, in order to close the recycling loop.

142 REPAIR AND REUSE

Rather than throwing out damaged clothes, make sure they can't be mended first. Even if adding a new zip or patching elbows is beyond your own capabilities, it's worth visiting a seamstress. Really damaged clothing can be ripped up to make household cleaning clothes and dust rags.

143 WAYS TO USE YOUR OLD PHONE DIRECTORY

There are a number of different uses for out-of-date telephone books. For example, they are good for raising the height of your computer monitor and if you have a compost heap they can be ripped up and added to it. They may also be shredded for use as pet bedding.

144 REDUCE YOUR JUNK MAIL

A significant amount of junk mail ends up on landfill sites each year. Once there, it biodegrades to produce methane gas, a major contributor to climate change – that's not to mention the resources used to make it, including trees and vast amounts of water. Start by switching to computerized bills.

145 RECYCLE UNWANTED PAPER

Recycling 1 tonne of paper is estimated to save around 15 average-sized trees. Recycle all your unwanted paper, junk mail and any printing paper you have. This saves energy because recycled paper uses 28–70% less energy in production than virgin paper.

146 BUY RECYCLED TOILET PAPER

Around 270,000 trees are flushed down the drain or end up as rubbish all over the world every day, according to the World Wildlife Fund (WWF). Buying recycled toilet roll will help to reduce illegal logging and boost the market for recycled products.

147

FIND WAYS TO DISPOSE OF OLD APPLIANCES

If you have to get rid of an appliance such as a washing machine make sure you recycle it. If it is still in good working order, offer it to a charity that collects white goods or a community group who may be able to use it. Otherwise, take it to your nearest household recycling centre.

148

REUSE OLD NEWSPAPERS

Use a log-maker or a plant pot-maker to recycle old newspapers. The main reason to recycle paper is not to save trees – because they are a sustainable crop – it's to reduce the loss of wildlife habitats as old forests are replaced with managed plantations.

149 JOIN A TOY LIBRARY

If your home is gradually filling up with your children's toys, why not investigate your nearest toy library? A toy library will help to reduce waste and save you money in the process. It's also a good way to meet other parents.

150 USE WASHABLE NAPPIES (DIAPERS)

Switching from disposable to washable nappies (diapers) can make dramatic savings on the household waste front. And if you can't face washing them yourself, look out for a local laundry service.

151

REDUCE, REUSE AND RECYCLE

These are the three main rules to keep in mind. Try to reduce the amount of household waste you create by avoiding packaging, over-buying food and recycling as much as you can. Reuse items when possible: for example, yogurt pots make good containers for seedlings.

152

GIVE YOUR MOBILE (CELL) PHONE TO CHARITY

If you change your handset, be sure to recycle the old one. Millions of phones end up on landfill every year. Many conservationist groups and organizations operate recycling schemes that raise money for specific charities, while phone companies and electronic-goods stores often have recycling bins where you can simply drop off your old phone.

153

BUY RECYCLED RUBBISH BAGS

Make sure you buy garbage bags and garden sacks made from 100% recycled materials. This will help to close the recycling loop and reduce the plastic waste in landfill. It also saves energy because it's much less intensive to recycle plastic than to make plastic bags from oil.

154

BE NEIGHBOURLY

Sharing your tools and DIY equipment with neighbours, friends and family is a good way to cut back on unnecessary 'stuff' and the waste it causes. There's no reason why everyone on your street needs to have their own workbench or lawnmower. This is also a good way to boost community spirit.

155

CREATE YOUR OWN RECYCLING SYSTEM

Make recycling in your home easier by creating your own recycling system. Use boxes that can be carried and emptied easily. Have different containers for materials such as paper, plastic, glass and metal and use stackable bins that take up less space.

156

PASS ON YOUR READING GLASSES

Thousands of pairs of reading glasses could be used by someone else but they end up on landfill sites instead. Recycle your glasses to help some of the estimated 200 million people around the world who need glasses but can't afford them. Visit Vision Aid Overseas (www.vao.org.uk) or the Lions Club International (www.lionsclubs.org) for more information.

157 PUT CARDBOARD TO GOOD USE

If your regular recycling scheme doesn't accept cardboard, it's usually possible to find a good home for it elsewhere. It can be broken up and used to prevent weeds in the garden or simply ripped up and added to your compost bin.

158 USE BOTH SIDES

Think carefully before you print – do you really need a hard copy of that email? If you do have to print out documents make sure you use both sides of the paper if possible and always buy recycled printing paper. Have a recycling bin handy to make it easier to do the right thing.

159 JOIN A RECYCLING NETWORK

Stop unwanted items such as furniture and electrical equipment going to landfill by joining an online recycling forum such as Freecycle. This is a great way to get rid of your 'rubbish' as well as to obtain things you really need, thereby reducing waste and saving you money. Visit www.freecycle.com for more information.

160 REUSE UNWANTED CARPETS

Carpets have a big environmental impact so try to get as much use as possible out of them, even when they're no longer good enough for your home. Use old bits of carpet to line the bottom of cupboards or the boot (trunk) of your car.

161

USE REFILLED PRINTER CARTRIDGES

Where possible buy refilled printer cartridges for your home computer. This will help to reduce waste and often they have the advantage of being cheaper than brand new cartridges. It's also important to send off your old cartridges to be refilled. Visit www.cartridgeworld.org for more information.

162

ALUMINIUM FOILED

Although aluminium foil can be reused over and over with no loss of quality, this generally isn't what happens and so vast quantities end up in landfill each year. Rather than reaching for the foil, store food in the refrigerator in old ice-cream tubs and wrap packed lunches in greaseproof (waxed) paper, which can be composted.

163 REDISCOVER YOUR LIBRARY

We live in a consumer culture but do you really need shelves and shelves of books and DVDs that you rarely watch again? Libraries lend CDs and DVDs and are a great way to cut back on your conspicuous consumption without missing out on the latest releases.

164 REUSE OLD ENVELOPES

Rather than throwing them out, recycle old envelopes with the help of a label. Even better, simply cross out the old address and stamp, clearly mark the new address and stick on a new stamp. Envelope reuse labels are available from Friends of the Earth at www.foe.org and www. ecotopia.co.uk.

165 DON'T BUY 'DISPOSABLES'

Avoid buying so-called 'disposable' items that are destined for disposal after a couple of uses. Razors, paper towels, nappies (diapers), wipes and plastic bags are often described as disposable. However, these items frequently use more energy than their reusable alternatives, so don't be fooled.

166 SWAP CLOTHES

Keep your wardrobe up to the minute by organizing clothes swaps with friends and family. This is a great way to socialize as well as to boost your wardrobe. And avoid buying a brand new school uniform for the kids each year by networking with friends with children at the same school as yours.

167 USE BIODEGRADABLE BAGS IF YOU CAN

Make sure you buy biodegradable versions of rubbish bags and freezer bags (although ideally you should use a reusable container to store food in the freezer). The same goes for nappy (diaper) sacks if you are also using them. This means that they will decompose rather than just sit in landfill.

168 DOWNLOAD MUSIC

With modern technology it's easier to download pretty much any kind of music you want to listen to rather than to buy the actual CD, or at least, download every other album you purchase. This helps to cut down on waste, as well as the energy used during production and transportation of hard copies.

169

REUSE YOUR OLD CDS

Are you wondering what to do with all those unwanted CDs that are hanging around your home? Recycle by hanging them in the garden or allotment to act as bird scarers. They can also be reused as reflectors in your drive.

170

CUT THE CATALOGUES

When you are out shopping don't be tempted to take a catalogue or brochure home with you. Most stores now have a website featuring an online version of their catalogue that you can access which helps to save paper and reduce waste.

171 DONATE YOUR OLD MAGAZINES

If your household gets through a lot of magazines, why not pass them on to your local doctor, dentist or hospital? Otherwise they may be recycled via most collection schemes or at recycling centres. Magazines can also be used as alternative wrapping paper and are sometimes appreciated by nurseries and schools who use them in creative projects.

172 TRY BORROWING INSTEAD OF BUYING

If you need a particular appliance or tool for your home ask around to see if you can borrow before buying. That way, you can see whether you really do need to go out and buy your own, which will help to reduce waste in the long term.

173

REPAIR BROKEN ITEMS

When something breaks, try getting it repaired first before you discard it and buy a replacement. In today's consumer culture we are conditioned to immediately replace items that could be fairly easily repaired. Even old furniture can be re-upholstered to give it a new lease of life.

174

BUY CHEAP, BUY TWICE

It makes much more sense to buy fewer, better-quality items that will last longer and perform better than to purchase lots of cheap things. This is true for everything from clothes to kitchen appliances. Cheaper definitely isn't always better, and can often mean that workers aren't being paid a fair amount for their labour.

175

DONATE BUILDING MATERIALS

Unwanted building materials such as rubble and mortar make up a large chunk of the waste problem. If you are renovating your home and have any of these materials left over, advertise them locally or offer them to a local community project who may be able to make good use of them.

176

RECLAIMED MATERIALS FOR BUILDING PROJECTS

If you are carrying out any renovations on your home, try to buy reclaimed materials. Items such as fixtures and floors are available from salvage and reclamation yards and often you can find far more interesting and individual pieces than you would elsewhere – and for less money, too.

177 COOL OFF WITHOUT AIRCON

While air-conditioning is great for cooling us down on stifling summer days, it also adds around 50% to the energy costs of a building, and used in cars increases fuel consumption by 10 to 14%. Don't rely solely on air con when it's not needed – open the windows when the temperature outside is good. If you do have to use it, try to use efficient systems and do use the thermostat.

178 CLEAN CARPETS

Before getting rid of a carpet simply because it is dirty, try hiring a steam cleaner. This will transform a grimy carpet and kill any clothes moths that have taken up residence. If it's really time for a change, old carpet can be used in the garden as a mulch to kill off weeds. Be aware, though, that you can't be sure what chemicals have been added to make even a natural-fibre carpet moth-proof or fire retardant.

179

IF YOU HAVE PETS, INVEST IN A SHREDDER

It may be worth investing in a paper shredder if you keep small pets such as rabbits or guinea pigs. You can use the shredded paper as pet bedding and the soiled bedding may then be composted in the garden.

180

REUSE UNWANTED BATHROOM FURNITURE

Unwanted sinks, soil pipes and even lavatories can be given a new lease of life as plant pots in the house or the garden. Use containers such as these to pot invasive plants like mint in the ground and keep them away from your other plants.

181

DON'T 'STANDBY' APPLIANCES

Research has revealed that 10% of energy use in the developed world is caused by appliances, such as televisions, being left on standby. As well as wasting energy, this also costs money so make sure you switch off at the mains rather than via the remote control.

182

KEEP YOUR FREEZER FULL

It takes less energy to cool a full freezer than an empty one so try and keep it topped up, preferably with home-cooked meals stored in reused containers. If your freezer needs filling, add plastic bottles of water to take up the empty space.

183 DINE BY CANDLELIGHT

Once a week have a candlelit dinner to save energy and boost the romance in your life in one go. Make sure the candles are vegetable-oil based, however, as paraffin candles have a much greater environmental impact and have been found to emit trace amounts of toxins.

184 PUT A LID ON IT

Save energy by cooking more efficiently. Putting a lid on a pan you are using speeds up the cooking time by around 6%. Always choose a hob size that matches the diameter of the pan and keep the centre of the pan over the element.

185 MAKE THE MOST OF YOUR OVEN

When cooking, try switching off your oven a few minutes before the food is ready and let the food cook in the remaining heat. Don't preheat your oven on a higher temperature than you need to cook the food – it won't get it hotter any faster.

186 DON'T GRILL IT, TOAST IT

Always use a toaster when possible rather than the grill (broiler), which uses more energy. Toasters also require less time to do the job than a grill and don't need heating up, so it's worth investing if you don't already have one.

187

SWITCH TO RECHARGEABLE BATTERIES

The average household uses around 21 batteries a year and only a very small percentage of these are recycled – less than 2% – which poses a significant waste problem. Another good reason to use rechargeables is because the power used to manufacture a battery is, on average, 50 times greater than the energy it gives out.

188

GREEN MULTIMEDIA

In these days of the iPod you can still be green and wired for sound – and audio too, for that matter. Invest in a wind-up Eco Media Player, designed by Trevor Baylis, the originator of the Freeplay technology (available from www.ecotopia.co.uk). You can watch movies or music videos, look at photo albums and listen to your choice of music or radio via this technology.

189

GO NATURAL IN THE OFFICE

Green PCs are made using low-energy components and use up to 75% less energy than a typical PC. For a green office, team your PC with a bamboo keyboard and monitor plus a recycled car tyre mouse mat. Visit greenpc.org for a range of new, refurbished and second-user computer equipment.

190

GET A HOUSEHOLD ENERGY MONITOR

These new meters will tell you just how much energy you are using in your home. They allow you to keep an eye on exactly how much energy your tumble drier and washing machine need to run so that you will know how best to save energy.

191 SWITCH YOUR REFRIGERATOR OFF

If you live in an area that has cold winters and have a garage, conservatory or outside storage, you could actually turn your refrigerator off during the coldest months and keep essentials such as milk and yogurt outside. Your refrigerator and freezer can also be switched off while you are away from your home for long weekends or vacations.

192 KEEP IT JUST COOL ENOUGH

The temperature of your refrigerator should be kept at an optimal functioning temperature in order to be energy efficient. This is usually 3–5°C (38–41°F) for the fridge and -17– -15°C (0–5°F) for the freezer. Check the temperature controls and thermostat by placing a thermometer on the middle shelf and leaving it overnight to get a good reading.

193 TURN OFF THE EXTRACTOR FAN

Try to use the extractor (exhaust) fan as little as possible when you are cooking. When steam builds up in the kitchen the best option is simply to open a window. Simple air vents fitted to windows that work by using differences in air pressure are a greener option than electric fans.

194 GREENER COFFEE MAKING

When you are brewing your morning coffee the best option is to use a cafetière – as long as you only boil the amount of water you need. The next choice is to use a stove-top coffee percolator, particularly if you have a gas cooker.

195 CHOOSE A GREEN ISP

If you have a home computer look for a green service provider for your Internet access and email. Find one that uses energy-saving business practices such as encouraging staff to use public transport and carbon offsetting. Visit www.greenisp.net for more information.

196 BUY ENERGY-EFFICIENT APPLIANCES

Around 20% of our total home energy usage is used to power electrical appliances, from kettles to computers. When any of these need to be replaced, research the most energy-efficient models you can find. In Europe, look out for the EU energy-rating label and in the US keep an eye out for Energy Star labels.

197

TURN IT DOWN

When you are doing the laundry, turn down the temperature on your washing machine to save energy. As much as 90% of the energy used is taken up with heating the water. By choosing a 40°C (104°F/warm) rather than a 60°C (140°F/hot) cycle you will use a third less electricity, and if you reduce this further to a 30°C (80°F/cold) cycle you will save even more.

198

A LITTLE BIT OF DIRT

It may sound obvious but washing your clothes less frequently will save a significant amount of energy. The average family uses its washing machine five times a week, which uses a staggering 26,000 litres (6,868 gallons) of water a year. Wear overalls and aprons to protect clothing while working at home.

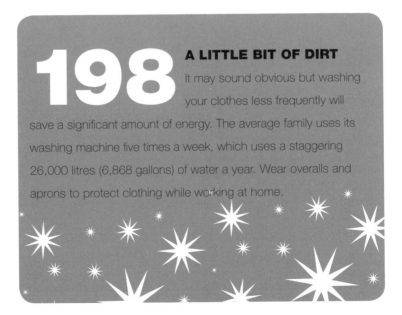

199

USE A MAGNETIC BALL IN YOUR WASHING MACHINE

These balls work by softening the water by as much as 70%, which helps to prevent the build-up of lime scale in your washing machine as well as the removal of existing deposits. They also reduce the minimum required temperature for cleaning clothes and the amount of detergent needed.

200

SWITCH OFF AND CUT EMISSIONS

The International Energy Agency (IEA) has launched a global initiative called the One Watt Plan to reduce standby requirements for all new appliances to below 1 watt. Research has revealed that some standby modes for televisions use two-thirds of the electricity than if they were switched on.

201 KEEP IT COOL

Avoid opening the refrigerator door as much as possible and whenever you do so, make sure it's open for as little time as possible. Each minute the door is open takes three minutes of energy to cool it down again.

202 SWITCH TO A GREEN ENERGY TARIFF

Green energy can be defined as electricity derived from renewable or clean resources such as wind and solar energy, and an increasing number of suppliers are now offering green energy tariffs. This is one easy way to help reduce CO_2 emissions and invest in renewable energy. The tariffs vary considerably and the 'greenest' are considered those investing in building new renewable energy sources.

203 TURN DOWN THE TEMPERATURE

Turn it down on your water thermostat, that is. The temperature for heating water should be set at around 60°C (140°F), which is hot enough to provide a comfortable bath. If it's any hotter than that, then cold water will have to be added to cool it down.

204 CHILL OUT

Defrost your freezer regularly to keep it as efficient as possible. Also, check that it is set at the correct temperature and be sure to replace any damaged door seals. Refrigerators and freezers should be positioned away from direct sunlight, cookers and boilers to keep them at optimum efficiency.

205 WORK FROM HOME

Working at home saves emissions from car travel and can be a greener option. If you do work from home make the most of natural daylight by positioning your desk near a window, which will also provide good ventilation. Research has shown that people working in areas lit by natural daylight have increased productivity.

206 LEAVE THE CAR AT HOME

Whenever you can, leave the car at home. The majority of car journeys are short ones that may actually be easier to do on foot or by bicycle rather than by car. This will also save you money and improve your health and fitness.

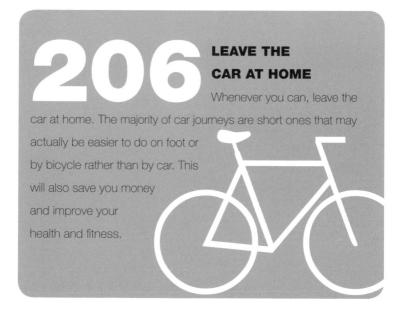

207 GET A BUS TIMETABLE

Pin up your local bus timetable somewhere that the whole family can see it, even if you usually travel everywhere by car. Short journeys are often easier by public transport, especially if you know when exactly the next bus or train is due.

208 DRY IN THE OPEN AIR

Avoid using tumble driers if at all possible – try to think of it as a luxury. Where possible, dry clothes outside on the line – they will not only smell better, but sunlight has a natural bleaching and sterilizing effect on fabric. If you must use the dryer, avoid overdrying and use the moisture sensor control if your machine has one.

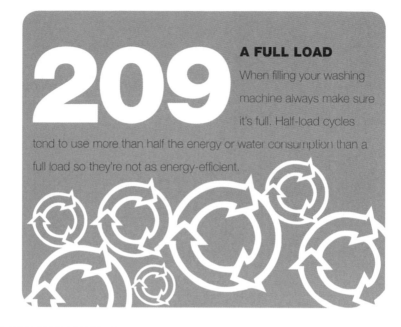

209

A FULL LOAD

When filling your washing machine always make sure it's full. Half-load cycles tend to use more than half the energy or water consumption than a full load so they're not as energy-efficient.

210

LOOK OUT FOR THE ENERGY STAR

When you are buying equipment such as a PC, make sure it has the Energy Star mark (see also www.energystar.gov). Products that carry this international mark, which was developed by the Environmental Protection Agency (EPA) in the US, are proven to be more energy-efficient than others.

211

REMEMBER TO SWITCH OFF YOUR COMPUTER

Appliances such as computers, printers and scanners all use energy so it's vital you turn them off when they're not in use. The general rule is that if you're not going to use something for 15 minutes or more, switch it off rather than leaving it on standby and save energy.

212

MULTI-TASK

If possible, have your home computer in a room that is used for other activities such as watching TV or eating. This means you won't have to waste extra energy heating and lighting a separate space just so you can use the computer.

213

GET WOUND-UP

Avoid the need for mains power or even batteries by investing in some wind-up technology. Wind-up radios, torches and lights are widely available having been introduced by the Freeplay Foundation, which developed the technology to improve communication in the world's poorest communities.

214

SWITCH OFF YOUR PHONE CHARGER

Make sure you switch your phone charger off at the wall when your phone isn't plugged into it, otherwise you are simply powering thin air. Around 95% of the energy used by mobile (cell) phone chargers is wasted with only 5% being used to charge the phone itself.

215 HAVE AN EARLY NIGHT

Rather than sitting up with the heating, TV and lighting on, why not revitalize with an early night once or twice a week and save some energy in the process? Reading with the aid of task lighting rather than watching TV under a bright light also saves energy.

216 ONLY IRON WHAT'S REALLY NECESSARY

Ironing everything from underwear to cloth nappies (diapers) really isn't necessary. Save energy (and time) by only ironing the things that need it. Is it really essential to have your underpants crease-free? Focus on the items that have to be ironed, such as shirts, and leave your bed linen alone.

217

SAVE WHEN YOU COOK

If you are using the oven try not to open it unnecessarily – an open door allows heat to escape and the appliance will then use more energy getting back up to the required temperature. Also, cook bigger batches of food that can be saved and reheated later.

218

GADGETS THAT WASTE ENERGY

Today we are surrounded by items such as electric toothbrushes, bread knives and can openers that use unnecessary energy. Traditional versions work just as well without the need for polluting batteries or mains power.

219 HAVE YOUR BOILER SERVICED REGULARLY

Inefficient boilers use more energy than they need so it's worth getting yours serviced on a regular basis to make sure it performs properly. If your boiler is more than 10 years old it might be worth replacing it for a newer, more efficient model that could save energy and money on your fuel bills.

220 WAKE UP TO AN ECO CLOCK

There are several brands of water-powered clocks available. The Eco Clock incorporates a digital clock, alarm, timer and room thermometer. It is powered by a water-activated battery that just needs topping up with tap water, so you don't have to worry about plugging it in or buying new batteries.

221

SAVE WATER WHEN YOU FLUSH

Flushing the lavatory accounts for around 30% of total household water consumption, and an old-fashioned toilet can use as much as 9 to 12 litres (2½ to 3 gallons) of water on every flush. So, if you are replacing your toilet, choose one with a dual-flushing facility that gives you a choice of a big or small flush.

222

FIT SPRAY HEADS

When installing new taps (faucets) in your home, put spray heads on them as this will save water. Make sure you fix any dripping taps as soon as possible because leaks can waste up to 4 litres (1 gallon) of water a day.

223

USE A WATER-SAVING DEVICE

If you are unable to replace your existing toilet, dual-flush devices can be bought separately and retrofitted to most toilets. Cistern displacement devices such as the Hippo the Water Saver or Toilet Tummy are another way to reduce the amount of water flushed away. Simply insert them into the cistern and save 1 to 3 litres (2 to 6 pints) each time you flush.

224

HARVEST RAINWATER

Using collected rainwater could save up to 50% of household water use – the same amount used to flush the toilet, water the garden or supply the washing machine. However rainwater harvesting systems best suit houses with large roofs and space for water storage.

225 GET A WATER BUTT

A water butt positioned under one of the drains is a cheap and practical way to use rainwater. It can provide all the water you need for the garden at least, which is considerable when you think that the average gardener uses 10 litres (2¾ gallons) of water daily on the garden.

226 YOUR TOILET ISN'T A GARBAGE BIN

Instead of throwing tissues, cotton wool balls and cotton buds (swabs) down the toilet put them in the garbage instead. You will need to flush the toilet more often to get rid of these items, therefore wasting unnecessary water. By being flushed, cotton buds can end up polluting waterways and beaches.

227

DON'T LET IT GO DOWN THE DRAIN

Put a container under the hot tap (faucet) while running it to save the water you waste while waiting for it to heat up. This can then be used to flush the toilet, to water plants in the garden or even as drinking water.

228

PUT EXCESS WATER IN THE REFRIGERATOR

Instead of letting the tap (faucet) run so that the water cools down enough to drink, fill up a jug of water and put it in the refrigerator to cool and have whenever you need a drink. This has the added bonus of allowing the chlorine to evaporate from the water before drinking.

229

MAINTAIN YOUR PLUMBING

If you have dripping taps (faucets) anywhere in the house, fix them immediately. Around 4 litres (1 gallon) of water can disappear down the drain every hour or so in this way, and up to 90 litres (24 gallons) if the drip starts to form a stream.

230

BOIL WHAT YOU NEED

Whenever you boil a kettle for a hot drink, make sure you only fill it with as much water as you need so that extra energy isn't wasted in heating unwanted water. The easiest way to do this is to fill the mug you are going to use with water and add it to the kettle.

231 FLUSH LESS

This may sound revolting but try flushing your toilet less often. One third of the average family's water use is flushed down the toilet – the equivalent of two baths per day.

232 REUSE YOUR BATHWATER

In summer, recycle your bathwater by using it to water plants in the garden. It can also be used to flush the toilet during the months when the garden doesn't need it. Keep a basin by the bathtub to make this easier and save the water you would use flushing.

233 TURN OFF WHILE YOU BRUSH

Turning off the tap (faucet) while you brush your teeth is an easy way to save water. This simple action can save up to 5 litres (8 pints) of water every time you brush, and if you make sure everyone in the household does the same, even more will be saved.

234 TURN OFF YOUR TAPS (FAUCETS)

If you don't have a dishwasher, avoid leaving the water running while you are washing or rinsing the dishes. This can use 10–14 litres (2½–3½ gallons) of water a minute – that's enough to run a small bath produced in just five minutes.

235

A SHORT, SHARP SHOWER SAVES

A five-minute shower can use around a third as much water as a bath. In a typical household bathing accounts for around 20% of annual water use and modern bathtubs hold around 60 litres (16 gallons) of water. Fitting a water-efficient showerhead, which costs around the same as conventional ones, can reduce the amount of water you use by 30%.

236

WASH YOUR CAR WISELY

Use a bucket and sponge rather than a hose to wash your car, as this will save about 500 litres (130 gallons) each time. Alternatively, reserve the hose for a final rinse only. You can also buy special car wipes that don't need any water at all.

237

NO NEED TO PRE-RINSE

Even with really dirty dishes fight the urge to give them a quick rinse first before adding them to the dishwasher. Just remove any leftover food and put them straight into the machine – this could save you as much as 70 litres (18½ gallons) of water per dishwasher load.

238

AVOID POWER SHOWERS

A power shower can use more water than it takes to fill your bathtub in less than five minutes, and three times more water than a standard shower unit in the same amount of time. Opt for a low-flow showerhead that restricts the flow of water and forces it through very small apertures.

239 REDUCE YOUR SHOWER TIME

Try to lessen the amount of time you spend in the shower. An average shower uses 35 litres (9¼ gallons) of water and lasts around six minutes. Try reducing this time and don't have a complete shower simply to wash your hair, which can be done over the bathtub.

240 DON'T REPLACE A SHOWER CURTAIN

If you are about to replace a shower curtain think again before purchasing another plastic version. Plastic production has a major environmental impact so opt for a glass screen instead, with the added advantage of being easier to clean.

241

WATCH THE WAY YOU WASH VEGETABLES

Save water when you wash your fruit and vegetables by doing this in a bowl rather than under a running tap (faucet). You can then re-use the bowl of dirty water on plants in the garden or even to flush the lavatory.

242

CHECK FOR LEAKS

Hidden leaks are hard to find, so it's a good idea to monitor them. If your water is metered you can check by reading your meter and then going back to check a couple of hours later that it reads the same when no appliances are running. If it doesn't, then you know you have a leak somewhere.

243

RATION WATER USE
FOR CLEAN PATIO

Rather than using water flowing from a hose to rinse down the patio or driveway, fill a bucket with clean water and use that, along with a stiff brush, instead. Even better, use some of the water collected in the water butt or recycled from the bathtub for washing down outside areas.

244

REDUCE THE USE OF
APPLIANCES THAT
USE WATER

Running your washing machine and dishwasher only when they are full can save you 750 litres (200 gallons) of water a week. Your garbage disposal uses lots of water too, so compost instead.

245 EGG-WATER GOOD FOR HOUSEPLANTS

Every time you boil an egg, make sure you save the leftover water for your houseplants. The nutrients released from the shell of the egg during cooking are particularly beneficial for plants – just let the water cool before watering them.

246 GET A METER

If your water is not already metered it's worth having one installed. Research has revealed that water meters make people more conscious about the amount of water they are using. This is also a good way to keep an eye on your consumption and to check for any leaks.

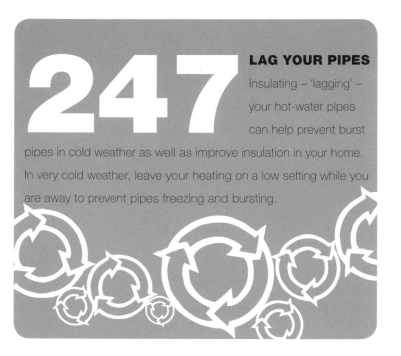

247

LAG YOUR PIPES

Insulating – 'lagging' – your hot-water pipes can help prevent burst pipes in cold weather as well as improve insulation in your home. In very cold weather, leave your heating on a low setting while you are away to prevent pipes freezing and bursting.

248

SOMETHING FISHY IN THE HOUSEPLANTS

If you have a fish tank, don't throw away the dirty water left over from cleaning it. You can use it to water your houseplants – it's rich in nitrogen and phosphorus, which makes it an excellent plant fertilizer.

249

CHOOSE 'A' RATED APPLIANCES

Make sure that you select the highest rated energy appliances for your washing machine and dishwasher to save the most water. 'A' rated appliances use considerably less water than other models – look out for the Energy Star and Energy Saving Recommended logos.

250

GO WITH A LOW FLOW

Fitting an aerator to all your household taps (faucets) is a simple and inexpensive way to conserve water. These devices save water by reducing the water flow and adding air to the water stream so that less water comes out of the tap during the time you have it on.